BRITISH SUBJECTS

Fred D'Aguiar

BRITISH SUBJECTS

BLOODAXE BOOKS

ISBN: 1 85224 248 5

First published 1993 by
Bloodaxe Books Ltd,
Highgreen,
Tarset,
Northumberland NE48 1RP.

Second impression 2001.

Bloodaxe Books Ltd acknowledges
the financial assistance of Northern Arts.

Cover printing by J. Thomson Colour Printers Ltd, Glasgow.

Printed in Great Britain by
Cromwell Press Ltd, Trowbridge, Wiltshire.

For Cameron and Elliott

Acknowledgements

Acknowledgements are due to the editors of the following publications in which some of these poems first appeared: *Ariel* (Canada), *Callaloo* (USA), *Cambridge Review, Hot Tin Roof, Independent on Sunday, Jacaranda Review* (USA), *Landfall* (New Zealand), *London Review of Books, New Writing 1* (Minerva, 1992), *The Poetry Book Society Anthology 3* (PBS/Hutchinson, 1992), *Poetry Review, Quarry* (Canada), *Stand, Wasafiri* and *Wilson Harris*, ed. Hena Maes-Jelinek (Dangaroo Press, 1991). Some of the poems were also broadcast on *Nightwaves* (Radio 3) and *Kaleidoscope* (BBC Radio 4). Parts of the poem from the film *Sweet Thames* (directed by Mark Harrison) for the BBC *Words On Film* series (produced by Peter Symes) reappear in this book in a revised form. Thanks are due to the Royal Court Theatre for the use of 'Granny on her Singer Sewing Machine' and 'The Barber' taken from the script of the play *A Jamaican Airman Foresees His Death*.

Thanks are due to Darwin College, Cambridge for a Judith E. Wilson Fellowship, and to Northern Arts for a two-year Northern Arts Literary Fellowship at the universities of Newcastle and Durham.

Contents

Granny on Her Singer Sewing Machine

You think you are a bird and your station is the sky?
Lick the thread and feed it through the needle's eye.

Are you an eagle or a hawk prepared to kill and die?
Lick the thread and feed it through the needle's eye.

When the enemy clips your wings explain how you'll fly?
Lick the thread and feed it through the needle's eye.

You hardly smell your sweat, don't fall for the old lie;
Lick the thread and feed it through the needle's eye.

PART ONE

Ballad of the Throwaway People

We are the throwaway
people

The problem that won't go away
people

The blow you away with our stories
people

The things have got to epidemic proportions
people

The we have no use for you
people

The blood we had to have was tainted
people

The loving we did wasn't safe
people

The needles make our arms look like sieves
people

The they look terrible at the end
people

The tell them s/he died of cancer
people

The priests are reluctant to bury
people

The buried at the edge of cemeteries
people

The keep your grief private
people

The world has no love for us
people

A Gift of a Rose

Two policemen (I remember there were at least two)
stopped me and gave me a bunch of red, red roses.
I nursed them with ice and water mixed with soluble aspirin.
The roses had an instant bloom attracting stares
and children who pointed; toddlers cried and ran.

This is not the season for roses everyone said,
you must have done something to procure them.
I argued I was simply flashed down and the roses
liberally spread over my face and body to epithets
sworn by the police in praise of my black skin and mother.

Others told me to take care of the flowers, photo them,
a rare species, an example for others, a statistic;
that the policemen should be made a return gift
crossed several minds – a rose for a rose.
With neglect, they shrivelled and disappeared,

people stopped looking when I went saturday shopping.
Though I was deflowered, a rose memory burned clear.
Now when I see the police ahead, I take the first exit;
I even fancy I have a bouquet of my own for them;
I pray they'll keep their unseasonable gifts to themselves.

Black Ink

Reading the Sundays I wash my hands
Four or five times. I never lick my fingers
To turn the pages; not since 1982 when I read
The Name of the Rose – the way those monks died.

More worrying than the splendid library
Being licked by flames, was the sight
Of a man expiring as he worked to quench
A thirst for knowledge that can't be satisfied.

My skin reacts against the detergent in soap
Forcing me to use a cocoa-butter moisturiser,
This in turn attracts more newsprint.
If unwashed, my hands would shine ebony,

No blacker. I note how yesterday my tone
Was lighter; how today, rain insists,
In a scherzo belted out like an old 78,
On blackening this city's red brick walls.

The news is hot, hungry, exclusive after
Exclusive with respected bylines,
Matching action-pictures and written in
Trick ink which disappears as it dries.

Inner City

The way a man lets his dog
strip the bark off a young tree
and the children of that man
break branch after branch
till the naked trunk of the thing
stands, a dead stump.

Who's to knock their heads together
now that the bobby on the beat
is part of the gang you meet at night
roaming the city's streets,
brazen in their uniform,
smiling through clenched teeth?

That same dog has slipped its leash
stripping a child's flesh
off her soft bones. Who can stop it?
Here's the police just when needed.
They tie a rope around its neck
(the dog's) cutting its steamy breath.

The children report the attack
as something miraculous. One says
he heard the girl's bones crack.
Another liked how the dog wagged
throughout. A third bragged
that after a while it was hard

to tell the colour of the ground
from the girl's smooth brown:
both were dug-up, both were raw;
both were under English law.
The children grow up feeling like dogs,
they worship stumps for gods.

Home

These days whenever I stay away too long,
anything I happen to clap eyes on,
(that red telephone box) somehow makes me
miss here more than anything I can name.

My heart performs a jazzy drum solo
when the crow's feet on the 747
scrape down at Heathrow. H.M. Customs...
I resign to the usual inquisition,

telling me with Surrey loam caked
on the tongue, home is always elsewhere.
I take it like an English middleweight
with a questionable chin, knowing

my passport photo's too open-faced,
haircut wrong (an afro) for the decade;
the stamp, British Citizen not bold enough
for my liking and too much for theirs.

The cockney cab driver begins chirpily
but can't or won't steer clear of race,
so rounds on Asians. I lock eyes with him
in the rearview when I say I live with one.

He settles at the wheel grudgingly,
in a huffed silence. Cha! Drive man!
I have legal tender burning in my pocket
to move on, like a cross in Transylvania.

At my front door, why doesn't the lock
recognise me and budge? I give an extra
twist and fall forward over the threshold
piled with the felicitations of junk mail,

into a cool reception in the hall.
Grey light and close skies I love you.
chokey streets, roundabouts and streetlamps
with tyres chucked round them, I love you.

Police officer, your boots need re-heeling.
Robin Redbreast, special request – a burst
of song so the worm can wind to the surface.
We must all sing for our suppers or else.

Dread

I saw these waves
roping off into strands
that combine to make a fat rope
breaking on mud banks and turning pebbles.

But the strands formed ropes of their own
and before I could name what they were
the ingenius head to which they were plaited
reared up from the tide, widening rings
that marked new heights on the South Bank.

Marley's unmistakable smile
shone through the wash released over his face
by the matted locks. He shook them free
and it was like the Crystal Palace Bowl all over again:
Bob under the lights, when, between chanting down babylon
he rattled his dread and in shaking them a tremor
ran up and down the city knocking points off
the stocks and shares at the Exchange
and noughts off some dealers profits.

He spoke through that smile at me.
'I an' I don't need anyone to speak for I.
Though you see dust where there was a tongue
I man still loud and clear on platinum.
Check your history and you will see
throughout it some other body speaking for we;
and when they talk they sounding wise and pure
but when you check it all they spouting is sheer lies.
Look in the river it's a crystal ball;
shout about the pain but don't shut out the bacchanal.'

Right then Marley start to skank
his big steps threatened to make the water
breach its banks, Barrier or no Barrier,
this was the dance of the warrior.
The more he stamped the lower in the water he sank
until his dreadlocks returned to the waves I mistook
for plaits doing and undoing themselves.

Colour

I woke with the last of my colour on my gums.
The rest had melted from me and coated the sheets
mattress and both pillowcases. I cursed myself
for sleeping nude as I stood before the mirror.

This pale somebody stared right back and right through me,
he looked so hard, I had to glance behind myself.
An involuntary shiver took me over.
Ghost after ghost hurdled my grave. I felt the blood

drain from my face. My one thought was, what would I say
to the cleaner? The dye in my black Wranglers ran?
That I'd pissed ink? Or that while I was several
shades lighter, his bedding was definitely brown?

I turned everything on that damn bed: mattress,
sheets and pillows and stood back satisfied.
My colour obeyed laws of quantum mechanics
no earthly equation or lab test could contain:

I watched it rise through that close-knit world of cotton
to face me once again. I bundled the lot in
a dark corner. My colour squashed like that became
concentrated; mopping up what little light spilled

into the room, it shone. What else was I to do?
Calling my shed colour to attention, I climbed
inside what was my own tailor-made boiler suit.
Airtight on me as before, I wondered how it

could have wriggled off all of me except my gums
and why. I took a bath deep enough to float in,
then stood at the mirror, naked and soaked:
the usual patches where I'd lost parts of me

in guest houses, from Land's End to John O'Groats
gloated back, familiar, ghosted and ghosting.

Honest Souls

What was it I pounded in an effort to crush?
Another's skull? Coffee beans? Peppercorns? Some wild bush
for tea or a drink that should be on prescription?
I don't know. Who was it that gave me assistance?
Whoever it was lay his big paws over mine
to help me, I'm sure and direct me now he's here.
Not liking it I switch to the part where I win
some bet and I wait for my winnings at a baggage
reclaim hatch, at a station I have no intention
of using, in the sense that the trains should all head
for the scrap metal yard and are trains only in
so far as school children on outings can mount them
and pretend to drive what is clearly stationary
because of wet leaves on the train track, you heard right
(not landslides, not rockfalls, not timber, but wet leaves)
or signal failure or five workers who did not
hear the Inter-City approach them and were sent
indecently early to their graves.
                                        Out of sheer
respect for them and in deference to wet leaves,
the station is closed for the morning at the least.
Oh there was that small matter of a bomb warning.
The luggage reclaim stands open for those who wish to
collect their personal belongings. The pounding
is nothing, it's coming from the kitchen where tea
and coffee – ground daily for public consumption –
can be bought in the café, closed today, for reasons
everyone knows are false. We ground-up anyway,
mine and those other hands that volunteered as guide,
in the hope that this time the bomb threat is a hoax;
that those five souls were not really hit as they screwed
tight the tracks; that the leaves will dry and roll away;
that today the terrorist plays with us and stays
tucked in bed, so we can sip cups of something hot
after all, and ponder the accident we find
ourselves in parading as civilisation.

Flying to Nowhere

A four-seater airplane I'm in drops low
over the Thames Barrier, moved to some
jungle-type setting, by which I mean
transplanted as places tend to be in dreams.

Jungle or not there's a cathedral – don't ask how –
in the middle of it, guarded by an army
you'd be foolish to meddle with;
dripping sophisticated weaponry, muddy from

a recent successful campaign, they ride in
to a town duty-bound to celebrate their return
in a mile's parade or capitulate. We (I have
company, three others, all destined for that plane)

run through undergrowth high as a garage, in a big
effort to stay camouflaged, reach the plane
I decide not to fly, acting as co-pilot instead.
This is when we land near the Barrier.

This is where we play catch with various sized balls,
in a green field that contains our mightiest throws,
green with care. This is how I come to call it paradise
and no one argues over the name and it sticks.

We buy our provisions in a nearby store
where the one language is a French patois
delivered with clucks on the upper palate
by the tongue, where the currency is English pounds.

My girlfriend cuts her thumb cutting a joint of ham.
I ask her to stand in a corner with her hand
in the air while I get through our shopping list.
There's no blood to speak of, but it stings all the way

back to the haven I'll call for argument's sake
heaven, since it's paradise in the sense
that we're all of us dead; we don't know
or we know and don't care; both feel the same.

The Barber

I farm mobile plots.
I am the deliberate bushfire
Killing in order to generate new life.

I thought a head was round
Until I started cutting hair on this base.
Hair on a skull is like clothes on a body:
Strip it off and you see all the curves,
Creases, bumps and dents.

Some heads suggest genitals.
Others take on the shapes
Of their owners' trades; in this case
Bullet-shapes, grenades, bayonets,
Helmets, trenches, maps.

One time I ran my hand over
A chap's head, the point on the back
So sharp it cut my hand; another time
I glanced at a fella's headtop,
What I noticed made me doubletake,

Stare harder, then long: the more
I looked the closer it resembled
Between the legs of a woman
And I knew I was lonely bad.
I cried on that head like a child.

I see the knots and protuberances.
I cut away to the baby in men.
I can read the fortune of a head.
If I look and I see nothing,
No hills, no bolts, no tributaries,

Then I know I'm seeing a head
With no time left on this earth;
It's like the owner's not there.
When I cut back the long straggly hairs
I'm shaping a wild plot to receive him.

At the Grave of the Unknown African

1

Two round, cocoa faces, carved on whitewashed headstone
protect your grave against hellfire and brimstone.

Those cherubs with puffed cheeks, as if chewing gum,
signal how you got here and where you came from.

More than two and a half centuries after your death,
the barefaced fact that you're unnamed feels like defeat.

I got here via White Ladies Road and Black Boy's Hill,
clues lost in these lopsided stones that Henbury's vandal

helps to the ground and Henbury's conservationist
tries to rectify, cleaning the vandal's pissy love-nest.

African slave without a name, I'd call this home
by now. Would you? Your unknown soldier's tomb

stands for shipload after shipload that docked,
unloaded, watered, scrubbed, exercised and restocked

thousands more souls for sale in Bristol's port;
cab drivers speak of it all with yesterday's hurt.

The good conservationist calls it her three hundred year war;
those raids, deals, deceit and capture (a sore still raw).

St Paul's, Toxteth, Brixton, Tiger Bay and Handsworth:
petrol bombs flower in the middle of roads, a sudden growth

at the feet of police lines longer than any cricket pitch.
African slave, your namelessness is the wick and petrol mix.

Each generation catches the one fever love can't appease;
nor Molotov cocktails, nor when they embrace in a peace

far from that three-named, two-bit vandal and conservationist
binning beer cans, condoms and headstones in big puzzle-pieces.

Stop there black Englishman before you tell a bigger lie.
You mean me well by what you say but I can't stand idly by.

The vandal who keeps coming and does what he calls fucks
on the cool gravestones, also pillages and wrecks.

If he knew not so much my name but what happened to Africans,
he'd maybe put in an hour or two collecting his Heinekens;

like the good old conservationist, who's earned her column
inch, who you knock, who I love without knowing her name.

The dead can't write, nor can we sing (nor can most living).
Our ears (if you can call them ears) make no good listening.

Say what happened to me and countless like me, all anon.
Say it urgently. Mean times may bring back the water cannon.

I died young, but to age as a slave would have been worse.
What can you call me? Mohammed. Homer. Hannibal. Jesus.

Would it be too much to have them all? What are couples up to
when one reclines on the stones and is ridden by the other?

Will our talk excite the vandal? He woz ere, *like you are now,*
armed with a knife, I could see trouble on his creased brow,

love-trouble, not for some girl but for this village.
I share his love and would have let him spoil my image,

if it wasn't for his blade in the shadow of the church wall
taking me back to my capture and long sail to Bristol,

then my sale on Black Boy's Hill and disease ending my days:
I sent a rumble up to his sole; he scooted, shocked and dazed.

Here the sentence is the wait and the weight is the sentence.
I've had enough of a parish where the congregation can't sing.

Take me where the hymns sound like a fountain-washed canary,
and the beer-swilling, condom wielding vandal of Henbury,

reclines on the stones and the conservationist mounts him,
and in my crumbly ears there's only the sound of them sinning.

1972

Year of departures
    and arrivals,
Goodbyes and hellos,
    big hugs and waves,
Promises and sworn
    affadavits
of the soul, across
    time zones and seas,
blood ties and wet eyes.

Rain sagged power lines
    after it rained:
miniature silver bats
    hung out to dry;
seamless pockets of
    light; colourless
tadpoles and targets.
    We pelted them
to see light shatter.

Light fell in sprinkles
    our stones loosened.
The ones we missed did
    disappearing
acts, fuelling talk
    about how each
had gone to heaven
    in a great hand
that grips a raindrop

between the index
    finger and thumb,
and keeps a raindrop's
    sad, teardrop, shape;
each one raised to where
    tired raindrops go,
where they never dry
    up or lose shape:
join us, we prosper.

Canard

The days lance
off windscreens
blindingly.

Nights fall hard
on distressed
furniture,

on our heads
soaked by pink
soft tone bulbs.

Dark glasses
are worn in
and outdoors.

Pigeons neck,
preening on
ledges ten

floors up. Come,
there is room
for another.

Kiss the nights
and days goodbye.
You're dizzy;

when those birds
push away,
follow me.

Domestic Flight

I heard what I took for wind chimes
3000 feet above London's lights,
each light a small sound.

The pearl necklaces of traffic
break, trying to get round
my neck of the woods.

The Thames ribbed and corseted
by traffic despite its peregrinations
in a black wetsuit.

Occasionally real diamonds startle
at high points in the city.
Gold is on the horizon, a rim.

Some distance below us an insect
with a compound look and rotating wings
hightails it home with bare ski feet.

The river is sanskrit in black ink
scribbling away into the dark,
turning over with each tide.

Greenwich Reach

My mind fastened onto the rod.
The fishes that are there answer

my hook's singular enquiry
once they have read the correct line:

'How do I know for sure you're fish
and not pieces of old rubbish?'

Typically, fishes reply
by swallowing the hook and bait.

The Fisher of Men is Old Nick
who wields a big death-dealing stick,

he wishes to rejuvenate
the Thames, not with scaly fishes.

He means to relocate people.
The question his hook asks doubles

as his hungry hook's sole answer:
'You really don't want to die?

You don't really have to die!'
Death winks at you in the water.

Take the niggling, needling bait.
Let your poor soul swim off the hook

as a fish, not like those big fins
stuck at Woolwich, too proud to eat,

too fat to sink to a sound sleep.
A fish's nightmare: to be in air

like the thinner half of a line;
to belong to a school whose day

never ends, like those stranded fins
floating in a giant soup, the Thames.

At Stone Ness

The river
bends back
on itself
as if
to assess
its own
considered
progress
or mission

The river
counters
this double
back move
with a twist
in an
opposite
chartless
direction

The river
sheds old
skin in waves
currents
and sea tides
a snake
renewing
reaching
perfection

Silver Song

I know little about water,
     even less about light;
all I see is the quick silver
     dancing there day and night.

I want it all in my pocket.
     I wish it was my bank.
In dream after dream I lock it
     up like fish in a tank.

Don't ask what light has done to me,
     or what water has said;
Not much, I'll say, they looked through me
     like I wasn't there, or dead.

Miles clocked up on city bridges,
     dawn and dusk by those shores,
countless flat stones found and skidded
     on water's polished floor.

Water and light, I must decline
     your invitation to me
to dive and dive again for coins
     that you two mint for free.

Sonnets from Whitley Bay

Troubled but not distressed.
FROM A WINDOW IN DURHAM CATHEDRAL

1

Stretches of this country smell so bad,
I apologise. We laugh at your, 'I'd think
About my love for an Island that stinks.'
Those hours we took to find the North had
Become a straight line: imperceptible curves
Broken by an occasional roundabout,
Until talk ran out and we banned ourselves
From idle thoughts of the distant South.

Wake up love. We've long passed the border.
The South is irredeemable. The slanted light
From the early summer sun is colder,
Now it casts elongated shadows of you and I
Ascending the stairs to our love-nest
Where we smell tired and unwilling to rest.

2

We always star in one another's dreams
In full technicolor and super sixteen.
We fall asleep like spoons and only turn
When one or the other decides to turn.
Morning is a silence that won't fracture.
An elbow-room closeness and the odd gesture
Confirms the other's thoughts in sea-air thick
With desire. We nod our approval at brick
In a city where I first said, I love you,
Climbing the cathedral's 325 steps to view
One shire shouldering the next, like molars,
As God would have it or Buddha, or some polar
Icecap and then the warming of the globe,
Exactly as the heat I feel when inside you.

3

These are the people I told you about,
The ones with mostly goodness in their mouths.
They treat us like old friends come back at last.
The pints you and I lever to nought renew fast,
Faster than we can toast the water of Tyneside.
Late into the evening we find seats side by side.
Our legs touch and when I shift it's to feel your hip
As I see it through this straight glass at my lip.

I've brought you here to be undressed by all
Their kind and hungry eyes, only to take
You to a Hi-Fi lit dark, Motown Soul,
And enough spring water by the bed to slake
The thirst of two flushed, open-mouthed lovers,
Through locked-eyes, locked-arms, hip-locked hours.

4

My love you fill my head to distraction.
I am pacing a room you hardly looked into,
Furthest from the bedroom-cum-granary
Where we lived and loved and woke in an aviary
That quietened as the light intensified
And objects muddled by the dark, clarified.
All that night nothing could come between us,
A sliver of light or dark couldn't separate us.

By morning the bed had split into half –
Us in a dividing current on two rafts;
Us in our deep dreams, private and sweet.
How did we drift apart, even in sleep?
One look from you of panic, loss, love,
And I leapt from my raft to share yours.

5

I hold up your 501s against my waist
To get the measure of you: come back, now,
From that big, big city that pulled you away,
To this one main street, coastal town,
With five minute jams and one of most things.
I knew between us, me and Whitley Bay,
We couldn't make you stay. We tried everything:
Flora and fauna, the sea's light displays.

Your long, elegant legs opened fluently.
I eased into a wet, warm, silky place
That made us gasp, quicken, then rock gently –
Our eyes searching one another's eyes and face,
When not one of ninety nine cars registered
Passing the house in the rush-hour was heard.

6

This kind of loving wrecks the body,
Makes it impossible to function properly.
You wake up mid-morning feeling like the night before,
But to go back to bed would turn your head forever.

You stay on your feet and sway like a ship
Becalmed, waiting for anything to happen, to slip
Your world back into orbit, but nothing does,
Except the light slips and you register a dull pulse.

The ship is hers and the sea is hers, the light
You see the world by, hers; the loving that night
Was all hers; the feeling that you're wrecked, hers.

The love you think is a blessing is a curse,
A weakness, something not hers, but yours: stop,
Before you have no pulse, before you drop.

7

Your touch, I'd nearly forgotton your touch!
And you've been gone less than a month, much
Less; yet here I am using poetry as hype
To conjure you from a Daguerreotype;
From a past neither of us could have known.
The fine tremor in your hands is mine now,
As is that chain of sweat on your upper lip.
I offer my China silk hanky whose tip
Sticks out of my top left hand jacket pocket
And a half-smile: take it, use it to mop
The sweat beaded on fur so delicate
It might be kissed away, not electrocuted.
All I can do is call you up and hope you'll come,
And pray that in calling you, no harm's done.

8

The miles between you and I open up.
The days stretch out against all my wishes.
I fight betrayal when a hand brushes mine,
Preferring a bruise from an upper cut
Delivered by one of Whitley Bay's British
Movement. A stranger's eyes make four with mine,
I hot up instantly like a four bar blues
Launched by Muddy Waters or B.B. King.

Not so long ago we watched a moon in a shoe
Step from that shoe which changed to something
We couldn't name, as clouds do, then the moon
Perched on a lake big like the sea; that moon
Looked like it owned the lake and all around.
But we watched it fall into that lake and drown.

When I turn my back on this North of Norths
And I kiss you goodbye, how come it hurts?

When sea-lit winds loosen a stinging rain
On Whitley Bay, your tears drown out mine.

This curved beach of seaweed and stones
Shows from my wavy footprints I'm all alone.

The waves form an orderly queue to see
Who's the miserable man bringing misery.

When those waves wreck in despair on sandstone,
It's my back breaking with my need for home.

I give up town and sea for glass and concrete,
And a capital adding to itself,

House by red brick house on the *For Sale* shelf,
And new-post-code street by tarmacked street.

Frail Deposits
(for Wilson Harris)

1. *The Trench Revisited*

We're being driven past when you point to
Where you'd pushed in a friend long, long ago,
Into what was a trench, to test its depth.
You say it taught you how a civilisation,
Feeling a blow or tug may still not know
A hand's involved, so can't feel indebted.
I was falling, horizontally, just
To keep up and lucky to win your trust.

Push him again, he'll fall on land that's dry
This time and think nothing of it, and you'll
Bank all that knowledge lifted from the sight
Your friend made clad in mud, convinced totally
That he slipped and your hand on his ribcage
Was your brave, unlucky, one-hand-clap save!

2 *A Jealous God*

The light on our first morning at breakfast
Is such that three women as many hundreds
Of yards away in pleated, cotton frocks as
Blinding as if the green, yellow and red
Are light sources and we're in some studio
Within touching distance of them; we look
Their way, quiet and still, more like study
Than look, they are grouped close, signing their talk.

The sun is a jealous God are your words.
Suddenly nothing means much anymore;
Watching those three women, a timeless world
Regards us as much as we regard her:
We feed like enraged Ugolino fed,
Though captive, on his captured jailer's head.

3 *Bone Flute*

'This your son?' enquires the curator
As we waltz in for our official tour.

You finger the thousand year flute of bone
As if about to burst out with a tune.

You tell how the bone came from an enemy,
Morsels of whose flesh is consumed by them.

When air is blown into the fashioned bone,
The enemy's knowhow and plans are summoned.

The flute I'm trying to blow a tune on
Belongs to you, got by me over years from

Stringing your thoughts sentence by sentence,
Or what must stand for you in your absence:

Having to check when I've said something
To see if it's yours since it has your ring.

4 *Seawall*

You explain rudimentary quantum theory:
The frailty of us jetting above weather
From one world touching down in another
With a wheel-screech equalling our surprise.

Ah, to leave marks in this life that survive!
That outstrip the skids of a jet's tyre!
The stretch of seawall we walk looks breached.
A man who seems too fit to beg wants change.

The sea is muddy, loud and creased in the distance.
We have to lean a little into a welcome breeze,
Our heads bowed from the direct beat of sun.

The soldiers in barracks reach us in waves
Dictated by the wind's direction and pace;
Dear God, I think, don't let this moment pass.

102a

1

Rain on the slate roof and more rain
collects in gutters then down drains.

Where does the picture come from
of it falling up? I hear a rhythm:

drips, slips, taps, smatterings, rattles;
out of this a pattern surfaces

that is thought itself. Then the thought
purely to do with rain, turns right

on itself, as if against all that water
washing the world, reverses water

up drains to rise off the roofslates
to where it's still, floats, and is weightless.

2

Cold in a room that won't be driven out
by heat, hangs solid like a gas lantern
or mosquito net or drapes or a web
dangling preciously in a strip of light.

I look at why it has settled for here.
The shape of the room is no longer room-shape
but the form cold takes settling in a place;
and I don't belong; heat doesn't belong.

I am no longer simply feeling cold,
I am being asked to leave, pushed out
by it into another cold, into the open
where size and blue puts the cold in capitals.

3

Early morning light weighs nothing.
          Lacking the conviction,
     it cuts through windows, but avoids corners;
filling the room with live shadows.

          The roof over my head
     takes on extra layers and new pressures.
I am instructed not to move,
          even a mere flicker

     could demolish this delicate balance.
The main beam is not the main beam I take
          it for but the very
     weakness I see and criticise in light.

I begin this apology,
          noiseless, urgent and scared
     that the roof might collapse and light fall flush
on me, and I might end up crushed.

Notting Hill

1

car-ni-val car-ni-val car-ni-val
this is car-ni-val

peacocks with feathers of the rainbow
wings' spread held all day

the robes of kings drag yards behind
heads-above-their-own crowns sway

car-ni-val car-ni-val car-ni-val
this is car-ni-val

bare-backed straight-backed princes
strapped to the steel pan and the bass

princess in a tassle of diamonds
glitters as she rattles her waist

car-ni-val car-ni-val car-ni-val
this is car-ni-val

freedom fighters in battle dress
the spirit of their banners in their dance

tinselled toddlers on shoulders
wide-eyed in the wildest of dreams

car-ni-val car-ni-val car-ni-val
this is car-ni-val

we reach for the rainbow
drape it across our streets
wrap ourselves in its colours

come let we wind and grind no girl
carnival not once a year
come let we wind and grind

we catch the morning bird's song
in steel pan and bass sounds
beat out those songs all day

come let we wind and grind no girl
carnival not once a year
come let we wind and grind

we bake fry drink like old time
the right amount of spice the right peas
the best rice cane rum and sarsaparilla

come let we wind and grind no girl
carnival not once a year
come let we wind and grind

Steel drums rattle and thump,
the sweating players jump as they play.
We follow the rhythm as close as wasps
their queen; sing the same few lines
in a sweet drone. The good follower
of a classy steel band knows

how to dance with each step:
put a foot forward, shake the body,
swing the arms from side to side,
thrust out the hips and smile,
if you're not laughing, part those lips
for breath if nothing else.

You're rubbing up another body
in front, one rubbing you from behind;
two on your sides bump to your hips'
pendulum swing. Wherever your arms stretch
for balance you grab a shoulder or waist;
when they jump you take off too.

Is so they carry you along,
they in turn carried by the rhythm
partly yours and everybody's.
It's ownerless really,
like this stomping ground
you can't see for people.

Never mind street names, they're postal
conveniences. Life is a honeycomb
made to eat; just sort out the sting
from the honey and the choreography
comes with ease, grace; so rock on,
but mind that island in the road!

The Body in Question

1 *The Heart*

A muscle, a pump...

Now that that's out of the way
Let's look at the heart's properties.

The heart is unquestionably
The chamber of love.

It quickens and reddens
At first sight of a receptacle

For its limitless capacity
To pour out love.

It contracts in pain
Far beyond the physical.

It really does bleed
When disappointed in love,

Opening these dark, little wounds
In the brain like clots.

Bare it in an operating theatre or x-ray
and all you'll see is a muscle, a pump;

But we who have loved know better.

2 *Navel*

A lover should clean yours to pave the way
for the blind inquisition of the tongue
(preferably the lovers' but not strictly).

Navels that are sunken retain thimbles
of bathwater which turns rancid then solid.
They get poked. Big stomachs push them inside-out.

Your love should use a reputable
cotton bud, manicured nails, excess care,
and talk throughout on everything and nothing.

When finished it is delicate again,
like the day the string fell noiselessly off
and was buried under the family tree,

or beneath steps leading up to the house;
so delicate, it's unable to sustain
the little kisses being planted there;

and baby-talk to the stomach to coax
those muscles strung round it, that take on ears
they seem that alert, to relax, relax.

3 *Hands*

If we had to walk on them
our perspective would be preoccupied
with ocean-beds and the earth's shifting plates,
with finding earth's centre, all at tremendous cost.

Not with space exploration,
not surface to air to surface missiles.
We would not clear a forest
because we would not be able to see

literally, the wood for the trees.
We would forage with the manatee and groundhog;
we'd have Olympics for the most hand-claps
from a hand-standing position.

We'd see God's face in a hand-jump
that could show both palms
long enough for us to make out
the broken Ms on them, that stand for Mankind.

that meet and merge
bridge the left side
and right side of the brain.

Bushy ones, thick
ones, are like hats
pulled low over the eyes.

They're not sexy
though the bearer
of bushy eyebrows is often

highly sexed,
and must pluck them
to study and pass exams.

Shave one or both
entirely and your face
becomes a big forehead;

an assault zone,
inviting slaps and jokes,
that shines with anxiety.

People who talk
with their eyebrows
have an extra dictionary;

we'd be foolish
to raise our own
and not join them;

especially
since they may become
Prime Minister one day.

5 *Buttocks*

Pert cushions with a limited supply of blood,
and heat. Buns that can grab.

They rob the high-jumper of that extra centimetre,
costing the world record.

They deny the ballet dancer that perfect straight line
while tucking in the tail.

An innocent slap on the backside is never
an innocent slap on the backside.

We would take from our buttocks to save our face
but not from our face to save our buttocks.

Buttocks are a source of worry for those who look over
their shoulder at a full-length mirror.

Thirteen Views of a Penis

1

A Buddhist demonstration of faith:
how much drinking water (uncarbonated)
can a monk draw up his untumid penis.

2

In an apartment on Manhattan's
Upper West Side a womanish voice cries,
'For God's sake, don't come!'

3

At a public congressional hearing
the prospective Supreme Court judge
has a boast about the size of his recounted.

4

In a house in East London in 1973 or 4,
five brothers ages six to sixteen are circumcised
on a table in a back room, consecutively.

5

The caption for a snap of a man whose penis
is wrapped right around one thigh
reads, 'He yanked it every day for this.'

6

All mothers in a certain tribe
pop into their mouths the penis
of crying babies to soothe them.

7

Needless to say it works every time,
unless there is something
seriously wrong with the boy.

8

A man who reached the North Pole
desperately wanted to pee,
despite a furious search he couldn't find his.

9

Flaccid, boneless, chesspiece
(a bishop), suspended upsidedown
like a bat in a dark cave.

10

Capable of growing up to thrice
its resting size, when stimulated
by touch or thought or praise.

11

A blueprint for most weapons
of destruction: missiles, guns
spears and sex without condoms.

12

In old age, when all else fails,
it may be the last thing left
to remind the old man of younger days.

13

We are living in the decline of the Penis Age,
You can tell at a public urinal:
a penis is always either too small or too large.

PART TWO

SOS

The suicidal soul and the homicidal soul beg on opposite sides of Forgive Me Street. There is war whenever they meet. They have missing limbs and missing teeth; they mash their fruit and mash their meat.

They got on very well once; they had an arrangement: when a homicidal soul felt particularly homicidal he or she would pick on a suicidal soul. This worked for a while, until a homicidal soul picked on the first suicidal soul who did not feel particularly suicidal.

There was war for days...suicidal souls forgot their suicidal tendencies; homicidal souls indulged homicidal drives. They fought with long, glinting knives and a wicked smile in all their eyes.

Pious souls do not wish to mediate since not one among them cares how those damned souls get rid of each other, as long as they do. Perhaps it will clear Forgive Me Street of beggars; so many beggars missing limbs and missing teeth, who mash their fruit and mash their meat when they can get their gums on any.

But Forgive Me Street does not clear and the war goes on between the two poor souls interrupted only by bouts of furious begging, when they tug the sleeves of the pious; following them, crossing the street when the pious cross; motioning to their bellies (empty) and lips (chapped) with mechanic's grease on their clothing (torn).

Then as if suddenly reminded they've a war to win they drop off following; forgiveness can wait. The suicidal soul loses that forlorn look; the homicidal has no look at all; both adopt a war-like glint.

Lucky for the pious souls their hands are too full to do anything about the fact that they are damned and must beg on Forgive Me Street while the pious are saved. The pious release a few blessings a day, glad those two souls don't get on; though they should and did and may do again.

Sound Bite

The marines look vernal
in the studio lights,
caught in their nocturnal
amphibious landings.

They patrol Somalia
in monsoon rains and sun,
far from the familiar
snowstorm-flashflood-season.

They shake the bony stems
of withered hands which children,
women and shadowy men
offer saviours not friends.

The local militia
in customised armoury
dash for the interior
firing at anybody.

Laden relief convoys
will reach bandit terrain
where the too-long starved die
anyway watching grain;

the last of the children
grown accustomed to eating
the bark off sparse trees, then
absolutely nothing,

can't swallow. They perish.
Here even shallow graves
defeat the healthiest.
All the words for food have

become the stuff legends
spring from, or plain foreign,
as these helmeted men,
fresh-faced in fatigues,

tarpaulin topped trucks drop;
who hop and skip from jeeps,
fit and fat and so proud,
to feast our eyes is sweet.

Hell

I hear the crows
crowing in hell
when they do crow
they do it well

they don't hit notes
they hit dumb-bells
only the grossest
make it to hell

dogs audition
to guard hell's gate
someone tell them
it's pretty late

they're too rabid
to guard estates
small bark or big
from mouths agape

what fruit juices
do the birds drink
to make their tunes
sound out of sync

like sheet zinc dropped
from a great height
or scraped or stomped
on out of spite

the same poison
rots all the seas
spikes eyes and skin
honeys the bees

the same carrion
sluices lychees
apples onions
potatoes akees

we're dead meat hung
on dead bone trees

GDR
(for Wolfgang Binder)

1 *Erlangen*

I hear them and I believe, what they are I know,
then I listen hard and they become uncommon:
birds first thing, hanging around my window
and every window in this town and every town.

They're puffy souls fluting about the properties
of the soul, gorging on pure sound this early
while sound is fresh-pelted and dew-flecked and free.

2 *Essen*

Refrigerator invisible in a corner
until now, now that the cooling motor triggers
with a fridge's intent and the whole thing shudders.

Keep the various fluids of my body cool;
keep silence below the temperature of a room;
keep stillness until ordered to do something else;
above all keep the temperature of what's real.

3 *Nuremberg*

I was on a road glossed by a recent downpour.
Streetlights, houselights, headlights and traffic lights
all finished stretched out on bitumin stretching away;
the freshness of it all seemed equally stretched.

When I stepped out on that road I was buoyant, relieved,
and obedient, I expect, to all the usual laws
still in play here and surprised, winded, dunked.

4 *Düsseldorf*

I didn't want to drag Hawking into it.
It was more a case of being unable to leave him out.
His example of all those monkeys hammering at typewriters
and one coming up with a Shakespearean line.

Where were we before that? God was on the verge
of having his existence disproved; the room was heavy
with rum-logic and intrigue. Goodbye God; cheerio Hawking.

5 *Aachen*

The time away was what I wanted and time was what
I got; plenty of it dripping off the ends of
my fingers; waiting behind doors that were opened
before and locked after me and solid as the best doors.

How long could this have carried on uninterrupted?
Not long. It was purely a matter of, well yes, time:
a door held for me and me not wanting to go through.

6 *Dream of the East*

The longest train I'd ever heard, that ended
in a sudden when I decided to take a peek at it.
A train that was there throughout my deliberations,
even those concerning its length and destination.

Getting up was a way of breaking the spell.
This I didn't know then, otherwise I would have
tested it: the moving train, the African thrown off it.

7 *Frankfurt*

The sexual revolution or something approximating to it
was going on in the hotel room next to mine; voices high
and low, muffled, thin and a drone then groan.

I didn't want to listen but where could I take myself?
It was late, I was tired and the room was just a room
until now, with me made alert against my will
and this event, not in my life, but there next to it.

8 *Now the Two Are One*

Stepback, stepforward; it was that kind of rhythm;
stepback, stepforward, to the reggae beat.
Stepback, stepforward and no one to stop you;
stepback, stepforward, so I could go on.

Like he went on, on the roomy dance floor
to the bassline and call of the DJ toasting
to the bassline and me thinking, join him, and then not.

Kite Years

A breeze swept sunlight
in waves from behind
cloud through the city.
Birds catapulted,
tumbled, fell and leapt
in these strong currents.

Trees were first to bow,
'Almighty please pass
in peace, all we have
is yours, there's nothing
more powerful here
or in all this land.'

Then torrential rain
followed. Gutters drank,
but not fast enough,
they gurgled and choked
and sank; roads funnelled
water uphill fast.

Trees pulled up a long
flowing skirt above
their ankles first, then
dripping at their knees
and in a final
revealing tug, waist-

high winds growled this out,
'Water, there's nowhere
left for you to cover.
Every corner in
the squares has succumbed.
You're all pervasive.

We remain standing
by your continued
grace, no one else's.'
Sun took up station
directly over
head, scattering fast

the last scrap of cloud.
Children played until
thirsty, coming home
only to drink, mouths
to taps. Water drained,
evaporated;

reservoirs became
mudbanks, then stark beds
their sole occupant
fled and left unmade.
One reservoir with
a dry cough managed:

'Master sun, I've seen
from my single eye
sunk in the deep brow
of a tall valley,
how you stood, ignored,
in the middle of

a field I mirror.
Your silent power
triumphs over all.
Nothing remains for
your unwinking eye
to outstare and dry.'

The great sun gathered
an entourage and
moved in a slow train
to the bottom of
the field it grazed in,
then to the bottom

of the world it ruled.
Flowers, already
thirsting for some rain,
wilted, starved of light.
The people's eyes grew
accustomed to sift

objects from darkness.
To the eyes of some
darkness remained hard,
distinguishable
only from the dark
of shut eyes and sleep.

All knew well what they
wanted; not one how
to ask. It would take
a child's innocent
request for daylight
and a little breeze

with perhaps some cloud
massed low, to see that
kite off the ground and
guess how high it flew
when measured by those
seamless, folded clouds.

Pyramus to Thisbe

The wall between our love
Stands as neat as foxgloves.
We whisper through a chink.
Our mixed breaths is our link
Doing what two lovers might
If the climate was right.

Deep and wide as an ocean
Between me and my woman,
Semiramis's wall is cold,
Dark, rough and solid:
Anti-love, anti-loving,
Anti-life, anti-everything.

But our breaths mix halfway
In that wall and must play
Out what two lovers would
Just do, if only they could
Meet and touch as we can't,
Haven't, mustn't, badly want.

We've met and done, my love,
All that lovers think of,
Except all's in our head
And heart, so, good as dead.
When I press against her,
She matches my pressure

Exactly, always; that thing
put there by those who think
love between us is a joke.
Let's show them in one stroke.
Elope with me my baby;
Be my midnight lady.

I am black and you're white:
What's the day without night
To measure it by and give
It definition; life.
We'll go where love's colour-
Blind and therefore coloured.

Join me under the tree
At Ninus' tomb at 3
a.m, everyone's asleep
Then, you won't hear a peep
Out of them. They will wake
Missing us far too late.

Us two, safe in some land
Where people understand
Love, whatever colour, shape
Or size it may appear;
Where they don't sling insults
Forcing our love to skulk

Underground, or as we're
Reduced to, run from here.
Meet me by that Mulberry,
Eat its sheer-white cherries,
Sample the nearby spring,
If you can beat my sprint

Or by a secret route
Reach there first, which I doubt.
I don't question your speed
(Since our love's fleetfooted)
Not seeing you, I speak
Unsurely, sound upbeat.

Thisbe to Pyramus

This mulberry tree
Leaning at the spring
Where you said, meet me?
Its fruit tastes of sin.

I stood there trembling
An eternity,
Or what resembled
An eternity.

Tree, fruit and cool spring,
That entire place,
Paled, paled to nothing,
Then just the big face

Fronting that lion
Bloody from a kill,
And smelling human
Flesh, made wilder still.

Pyramus, I swear
I ran faster than
You, into a cave.
It fell from my hand...

I would have turned back
For that crucial shawl
Risking my own neck,
Than you find it mauled

And, thinking me dead
From all that fresh blood
And fabric in shreds,
Run, run yourself through!

Death's the wall between
Us now; the wall seen
From life, none can see
Unless death agrees.

How fast you scaled that!
Who's to win this race?
You, for your swift death
Sure I was savaged?

Or me seeing this:
You, all warm, bloody,
And knowing the gist
Of it's you loved me?

Your wet blade's sweet tip
Is hardly in me;
Already the fruit
Turn red on the tree.